THE MONARCHS

OF CAPE MAY POINT

Pecki Sherman Witonsky

© 2016 Pecki Sherman Witonsky

ISBN: 978-1717390578
Library of Congress Control Number: 2016937707

Printed in the United States of America

MONARCH X-ING sign by Samm Wehman Epstein

CONTENTS

INTRODUCTION

THE MARVELOUS NATURAL HISTORY OF THE MONARCH

The monarch is one of the most beautiful and regal of butterflies, which is why its name means king and queen. It also has one of the most interesting multigenerational life cycles in the butterfly world. In March, the generation of monarchs that survived the winter in Mexico migrate to the southern U.S. where they mate and females lay their eggs on milkweeds. The caterpillars that are born go through a fascinating metamorphosis, emerging as butterflies. These monarchs, the first generation of the new year, fly further north in search of milkweeds to lay eggs for another generation.

In late spring and summer, two or three more generations of monarchs arrive in our local gardens in search of flowers for nectaring and milkweeds for their eggs. In late summer and early fall, another generation of monarch butterflies migrates through our community. Some of them will be members of the generation that lives through the winter. Others will mate again and lay eggs for those monarchs who will reach Mexico.

During their stay with us, the monarchs generate a great deal of interest from naturalists, school children and gardeners.

HERE IS THE STORY, IN PICTURES, of how an elementary school and a community came together to do their part to help the monarch butterflies.

Spring

IT WAS a long, cold and lonely winter
for the lighthouse.

Now spring is here and there is a lot to see.

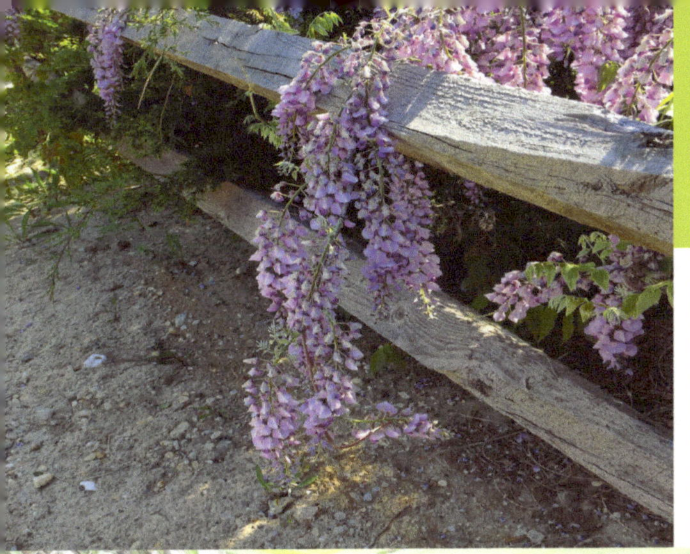

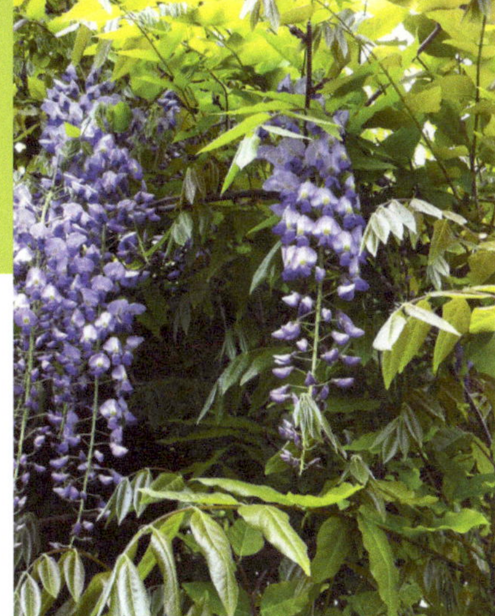

The lighthouse loves seeing the wild draping wisteria.

It knows it is time to start looking for the milkweed plants.

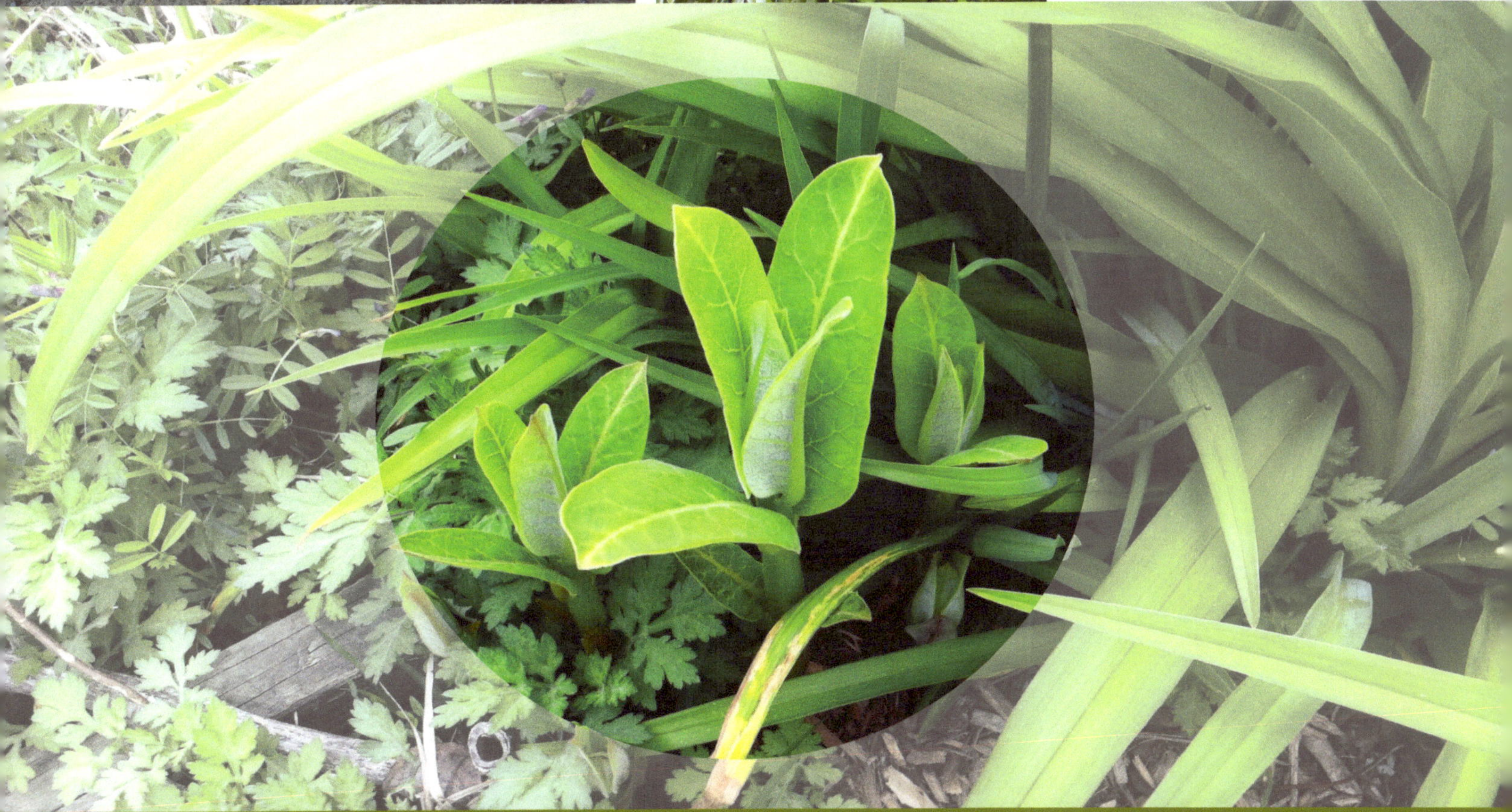

THE MILKWEED CALLS TO THE LIGHTHOUSE, "I'M PUSHING UP. IT WILL BE EASY FOR THE MONARCHS TO FIND ME."

students at Cape May
Elementary School
plant milkweed to welcome
the monarchs that arrive here
during late spring,
summer and fall.

PLANTING MILKWEED

Milkweed seedlings

PLANTING MILKWEED

Butterfly Weed

Tropical Milkweed

TYPES OF MILKWEED

Swamp Milkweed

Common Milkweed

THESE ARE TYPES OF MILKWEED THAT CAN BE PLANTED IN THE SPRING.

Milkweed Growth Cycle

SUMMER

BUTTERFLY GARDENS

BUTTERFLY
GARDEN

BUTTERFLIES

1

2

3

4

5

6

AND MORE!

CAN YOU IDENTIFY THESE ANIMALS?

ANSWERS

1) Ruby-throated hummingbird
2) Bumblebee
3) Saddlebag dragonfly
4) Needham's skimmer
5) Widow skimmer
6) Great egret
7) Halloween pennant
8) Sandpiper
9) Eastern mud turtle
10) Mallard ducks
11) Marsh Wren
12) Male blue-faced meadowhawk

OTHER SUMMER RESIDENTS ALSO BENEFIT FROM THE NATURAL AREAS HERE

FALL

THE LIGHTHOUSE IS HAPPY TO SEE THE ROSEMALLOW IN BLOOM. IT MEANS THE MONARCHS WILL BE COMING THROUGH IN GREAT NUMBERS.

LOOK, THEY ARE HERE!

LIFE CYCLE

GOING THRU THE STAGES

From laying her eggs on a milkweed plant, to caterpillar, to chrysalis, to emergence as a monarch butterfly takes about thirty days.

DAY 1

Lady Monarch lays her eggs on the underside of the milkweed leaf.

DAY 3 OR 4

The tiny caterpillar (instar) emerges, all the while eating milkweed leaves- its only food source while busily shedding its skin 5 times until it becomes a full grown caterpillar on day 18. That same day.........

DAY 18

The caterpillar hangs in a "J" position, building its chrysalises.

DAYS 18 TO 29

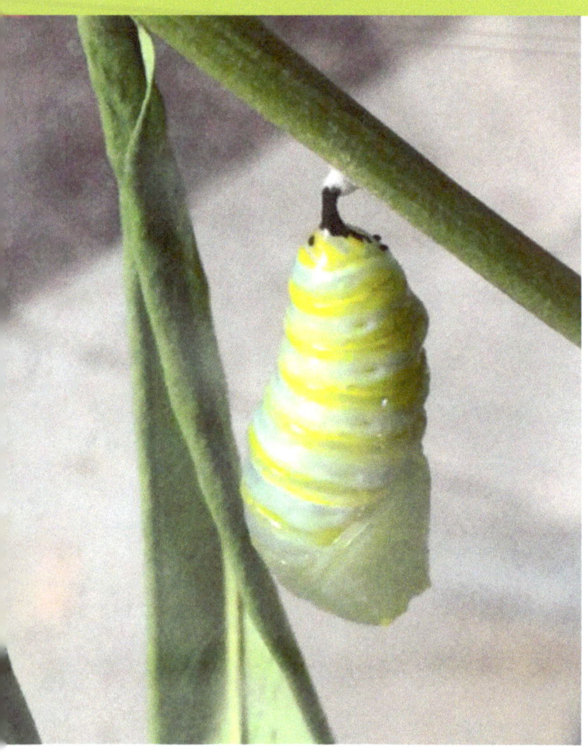

Metamorphosis – the time it takes for the caterpillar to change from a caterpillar into a butterfly

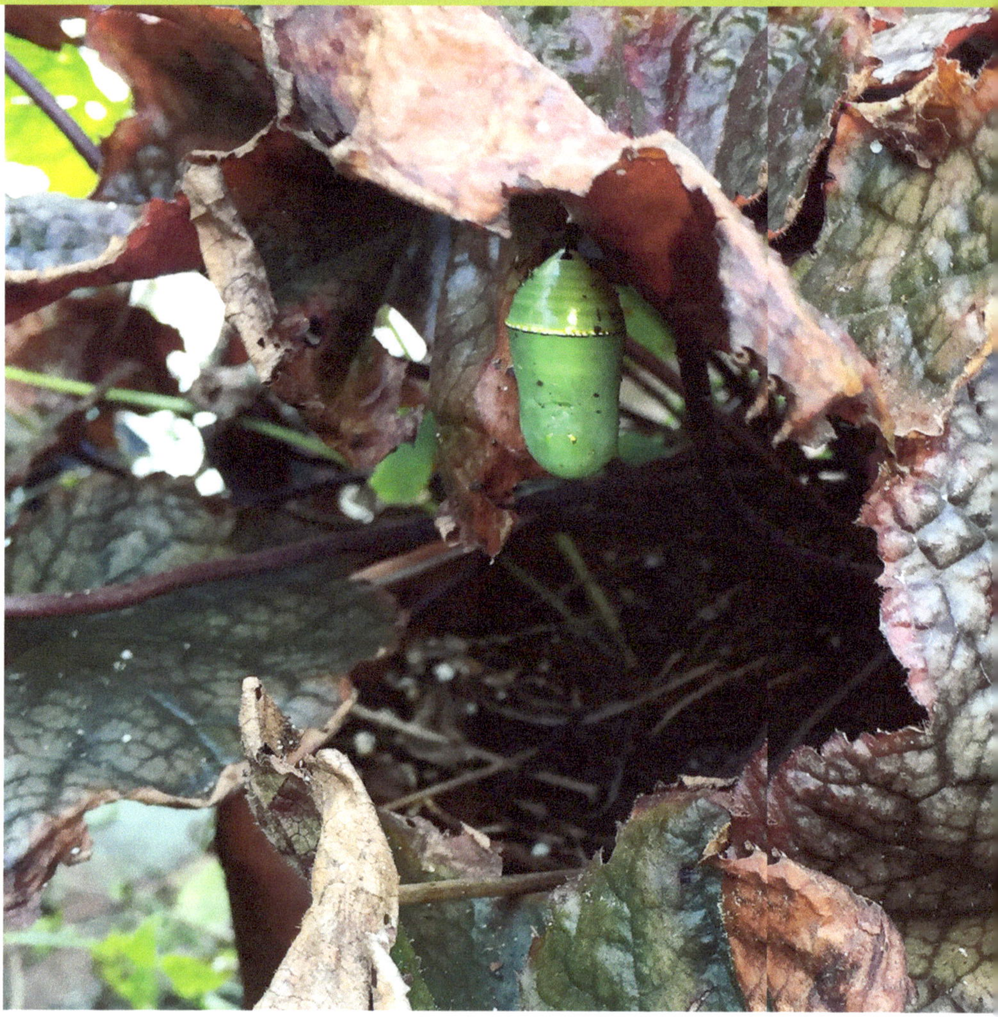

Chrysalis hidden in the coralbell plant

LIFE CYCLE

The Chrysalis can be hard to find!

LIFE CYCLE

DAY 30
A full-grown monarch butterfly emerges.

After the monarch butterfly emerges from its chrysalis it can nectar on all the flowers in the garden.

LIFE CYCLE

NECTARING

Gathering together before dark.

LIFE CYCLE

ROOSTING

The pyracantha is in full berry. It is time for the monarchs to leave, fly over the dunes and go south.

LIFE CYCLE

LIFE CYCLE

VOLÁ CON SEGURIDAD!"

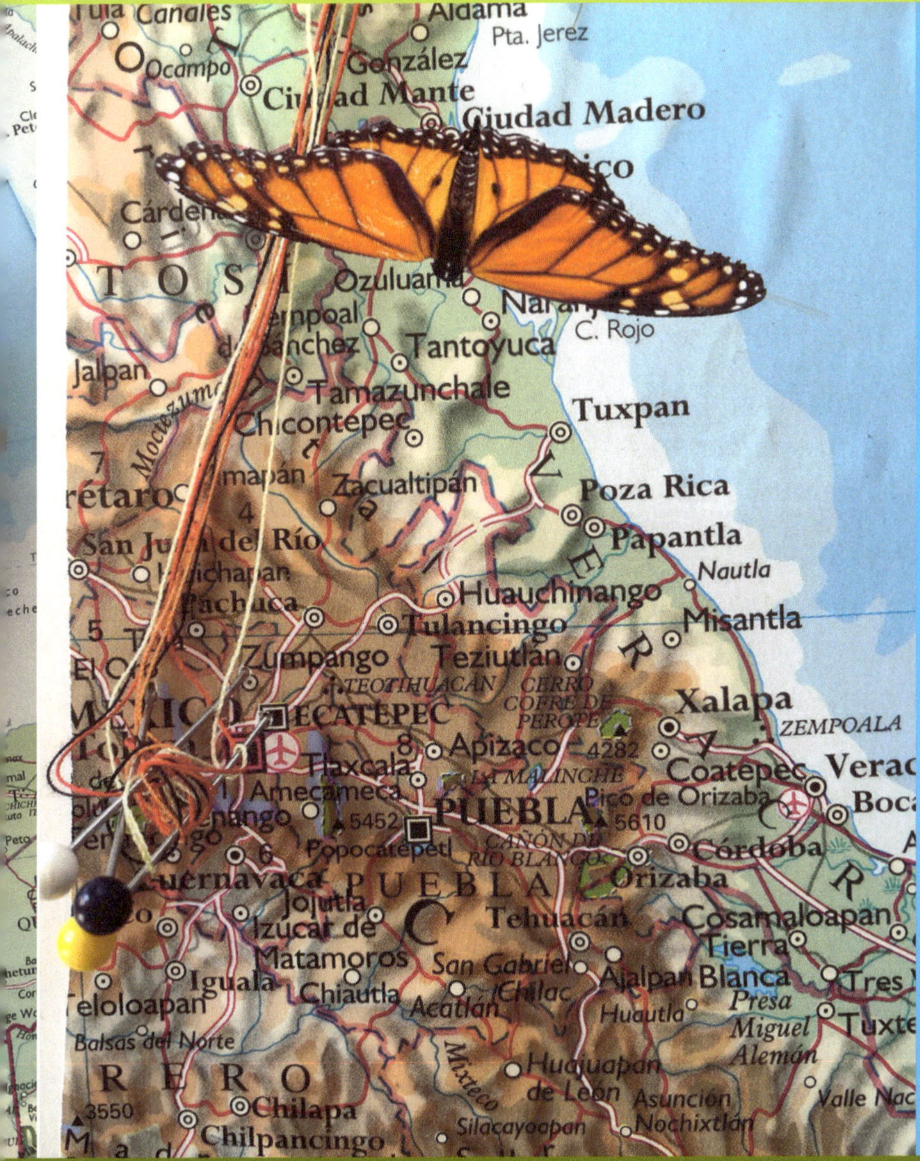

In Mexico,
the arriving monarchs will hear,
"Welcome monarch butterflies –
Mariposas monarca de bienvenida."

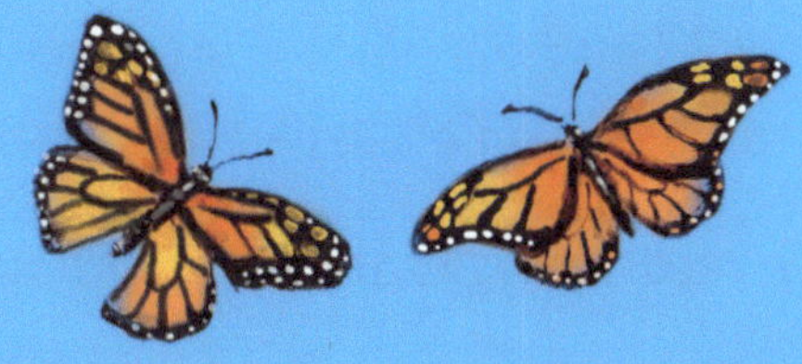

TAG AND RELE

WHY WE TAG MONARCHS

We are tagging the monarchs so that we can monitor the migration. It is similar to banding birds.

HOW TO TAG

Monarch tags are supplied through Monarch Watch. Each tag has its own number name, such as KG123, a telephone number, and an email address. The tag weighs 0.0006th of a gram. A Monarch butterfly weighs ½ gram or 0.5 gram

When the butterfly is feeding on a plant it is fairly easy to catch it up in a net. We carefully take it out of the net and place the tag on its left lower wing. Then we make a note of number KG123 and the place it is tagged, like Cape May Point, and note if it is a male or a female. A male has an enlarged dark spot on his wing.

We record this information in our notebooks.

At the end of the season in CMP, all lists are compiled in a data file. This list can be shared with Monarch Watch.

We now know about migration routes, possible travel time and can make sure the milkweed is maintained for the butterflies.

If KG123 is later found (dead or alive) in Virginia, or Texas or Mexico, because of its number it can be traced back to where it was originally tagged.

All this information is very valuable to scientists and fun for us to know.

My neighbors, Julia and her brothers, mapped the Monarch migration (using data collected by the Monarch Monitoring Project) from Cape May Point, down the east coast of the United States to the El Rosario preserve in Mexico. That same fall the children joined in the tagging and releasing.

Tag and Release

Julia tagging and releasing

Tag and Release

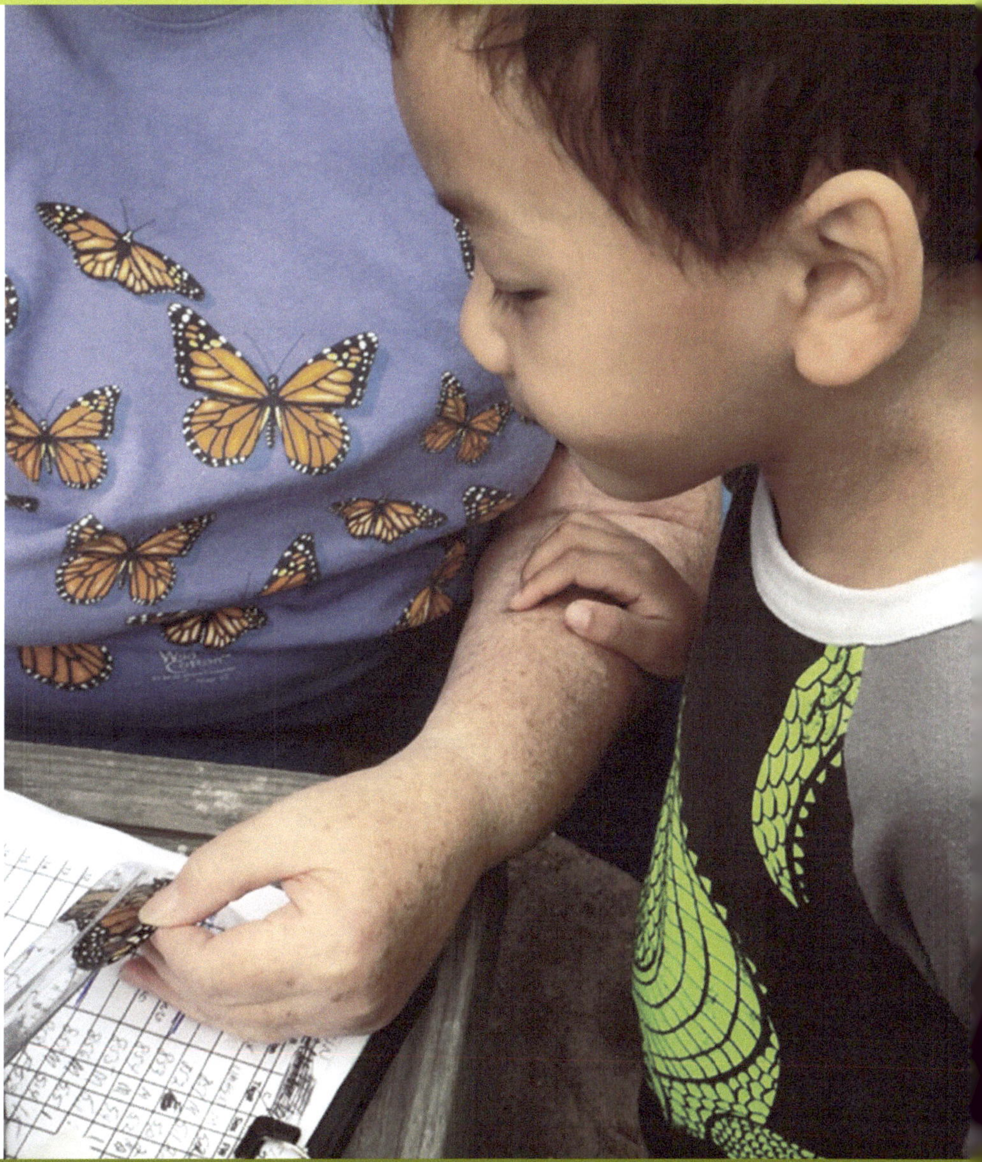

AJ is watching.

TWORK
53

LOWER GRADES

STUDENTS LEARN ABOUT MONARCHS AND CREATE ART TO CELEBRATE THEIR RETURN.

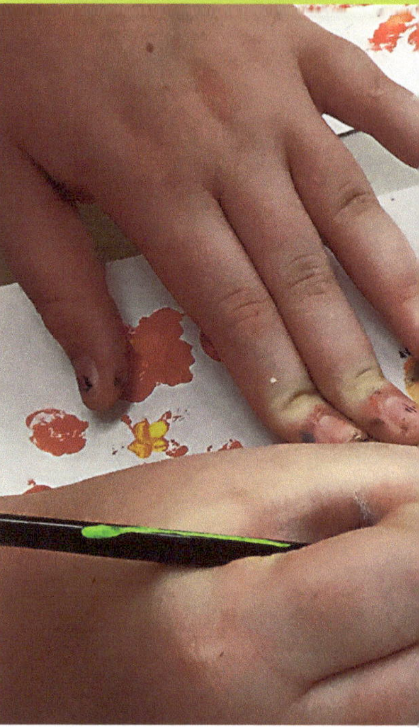

UPPER GRADES

KILL
TOUGH
WEEDS
WITHOUT HANDLING
KILLS
The ROOTS!
GLYPHOSATE
READY-TO-USE
POISON IVY &
TOUGH BRUSH KILLER PLUS
RAINPROOF
IN 30 MINUTES!
CAUTION

Use of Herbicides (Glyphosate)

Loss of Habitat

Two environmental issues that impact the monarchs

WE CAN HELP THE MONARCH BUTTERFLY SURVIVE BY PLANTING MILKWEEDS

The monarch butterfly is facing a combination of threats to its very existence.

There are efforts here to have it placed on the endangered species list.

In the United States, increasing land development destroys natural habitats beneficial to the monarch and the use of pesticides and herbicides is killing native plants, like milkweeds. Milkweeds are the only plant hosts that Mother Nature provides for the monarch butterfly to reproduce. In Mexico, deforestation and illegal logging in the high mountain preserves – the Monarch's wintering grounds – cause a great loss in their numbers. Here in the Cape May Point community we do what we can do by acting locally to contribute to this global rescue mission.

We benefit immensely from the work of The Monarch Monitoring Project (MMP), established in 1990, which is a research and education program of New Jersey Audubon's Cape May Bird Observatory focusing on the fall migration of monarch butterflies along the Atlantic coast. For over two decades the MMP—along with its founder, Dick Walton; Director, Mark Garland; Field Coordinator, Louise Zemaitis; Scientific Advisor, Dr. Lincoln Brower—has gathered data on monarchs moving through Cape May during September and October. MMP staff and volunteers also conduct informational programs on monarch biology and tagging.

As naturalists, gardeners, school children and community, we love our monarchs. Therefore, we plant colorful, fragrant butterfly gardens filled with flowers for nectaring and lots of milkweeds where Lady Monarch can lay her eggs and for the newly emerging caterpillars to feed upon.

WE ARE FORTUNATE TO HAVE MONARCHS CROSSING THROUG OUR SMALL COMMUNITY. COORDINATES OF CAPE MAY POINT, NJ

LATITUDE 38° 56′ N
LONGITUDE 74° 57′ W

RESOURCES

RESOURCES MONARCH MONITORING PROJECT
www.monarchmonitoringproject.com

NEW JERSEY AUDUBON
www.njaudubon.org

PESTICIDES AND YOU
www.beyondpesticides.org

NATURAL RESOURCES DEFENSE COUNCIL
www.nrdc.org "Monarch Butterflies Get Their Day In Court"

MONARCH WATCH
www.monarchwatch.org http://monarchwatch.org/bring-back-the-monarchs/ "Bring Back the Monarchs and Milkweeds"

EARTHJUSTICE
www.earthjustice.org

SCIENCE DAILY
www.sciencedaily.com

FOOD & WATER WATCH
www.foodandwaterwatch.org

NOVA ON PBS
"The Incredible Journey of the Butterflies"

NOW GET MILKWEED SEEDS FROM A FRIEND OR GO TO YOUR LOCAL NATURE CENTER OR GARDEN SHOP TO BUY MILKWEED SEEDLINGS. SHARE THEM. THEN GO TO YOUR LOCAL LIBRARY OR BOOKSTORE TO ENJOY THE MANY BOOKS ON MONARCH BUTTERFLIES.

Special Thanks To

Alice and Julia Gibson, Sharon Fruchtman, Sandy Sandmeyer-Bryan *and the students in Cape May City Elementary School. I enjoyed every day we spent together.*

Alexandra Witonsky *for Spanish translations.*

Lynn Lee, *you generously supplied us with milkweed plants, your time, and expertise.*

Millie Morgan, Edie Schuhl, Lee Shupert *and all the gardeners in Cape May Point who invite the monarch butterflies into their lives.*

The Monarch Monitoring Project staff *and interns, our teachers.*

Photos: *Pecki Sherman Witonsky, Alice Gibson, Jerri Hodby, Seth Witonsky, Lu Ann Daniels, Ron Rollet.*

Lighthouse photo on pg 8 By Ryan Linton - Own work, CC BY-SA 3.0, https://commons.wikimedia.org/w/index.php?curid=21076214